My
Reading
List

This book was given to

_____

by

_____

on this date

_____

My goal is to read

_____
(amount)
books!

MY READING LIST
A Child's Personal Reading Record

Created by
Emily Ellison

"There have been societies that did not use the wheel,
but there have been no societies that did not tell stories."

— Ursula K. LeGuin
The Language of the Night

For
Elli, April, and Patch

I want to thank the staff of the Children's Department of the Atlanta-Fulton County Public Library's Buckhead Branch for their suggestions, assistance, and kindness and the folks at Lemuria, in Jackson, Mississippi, who gave me my first copies of *Uncle Elephant* and *Frog and Toad.*

— E.E.

Published by LONGSTREET PRESS, INC.,
a subsidiary of Cox Newspapers,
a subsidiary of Cox Enterprises, Inc.
2140 Newmarket Parkway
Suite 122
Marietta, Georgia 30067

Printed in the United States of America

2nd printing, 1997

Library of Congress Catalog Number 94-74238

ISBN: 1-56352-205-5

This book was printed by Western Publishing Co. Inc., Racine, Wisconsin

Cover & book design by Neil Hollingsworth

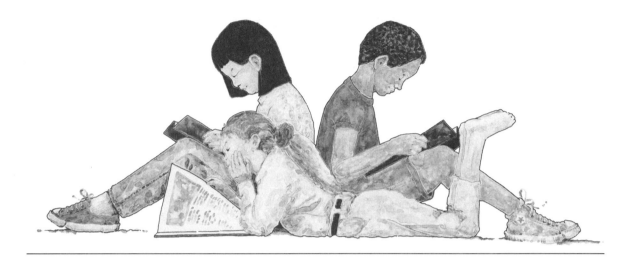

A NOTE TO PARENTS

Children who are the best readers generally become the best students. And the best way to create great readers is by starting at an early age reading aloud to them. At the back of the book are other simple suggestions for encouraging children to read and for developing their skills. There are also three reading lists — one for beginning readers (ages 4-7), progressing readers (ages 5-9), and advanced readers (ages 8-12).

Contrary to what many people think, there is no shortage of truly wonderful children's literature; the tough job is knowing where to begin with so many books on the market. These lists may help get you started if you're not familiar with children's books. But they're meant only as that — starters; there are many award-winning and best-selling books not included simply because they did not appeal greatly to me. All libraries and most good book stores can give you the list of Caldecott and Newberry Award winners (the prizes given annually to a committee's choice of the best illustrator and author, respectively, for a particular year). They can also give you lists of the annual Coretta Scott King Awards (given to African-American artists and writers), Reading Rainbow books, and often the suggested reading lists of local public and private schools.

The main thing about reading with children, however, has less to do with award-winners and library lists. It has to do with giving children a lifelong love of words and books and discovering lives and worlds they would never know without them. And, if you and your child have never read a book by Arnold Lobel or Eleanor Estes or William Steig or Natalie Babbitt, you're in for a treat!

My Reading List

Books I Have Read

Name of Book:	
Author:	Date Read:
	AWARD Sticker!

Name of Book:	
Author:	Date Read:
	AWARD Sticker!

Name of Book:	
Author:	Date Read:
	AWARD Sticker!

Name of Book:	
Author:	Date Read:
	AWARD Sticker!

Name of Book:	
Author:	Date Read:
	AWARD Sticker!

Books I Have Read

Name of Book:		
....		AWARD Sticker!
Author:	Date Read:	

Name of Book:		
....		AWARD Sticker!
Author:	Date Read:	

WILLIAM STEIG, the author of ***Sylvester and the Magic Pebble, Dr. DeSoto, Brave Irene***, and many other famous children's books, did not publish his first book until he was sixty-one years old!

Name of Book:		
....		AWARD Sticker!
Author:	Date Read:	

Name of Book:		
....		AWARD Sticker!
Author:	Date Read:	

I like to read books about . . . ☑

- ❏ adventure
- ❏ animals
- ❏ artists
- ❏ dinosaurs
- ❏ fairy tales
- ❏ famous people
- ❏ ghosts and monsters
- ❏ history
- ❏ kings and queens

- ❏ mermaids
- ❏ myths
- ❏ nature
- ❏ other kids
- ❏ pets
- ❏ pirates
- ❏ science/scientists
- ❏ space and planets
- ❏ sports

❏ _____

Books I Have Read

Name of Book:

....

Author: Date Read:

AWARD
Sticker!

Name of Book:

....

Author: Date Read:

AWARD
Sticker!

So far I have read _____ books!

Name of Book:

....

Author: Date Read:

AWARD
Sticker!

Name of Book:

....

Author: Date Read:

AWARD
Sticker!

Books I Have Read

Name of Book:

....

Author:

Date Read:

AWARD
Sticker!

Name of Book:

....

Author:

Date Read:

AWARD
Sticker!

If a friend asked me to recommend a book, I would tell my friend to read:

_____

I think this is a great book because:

_____

_____

_____

_____

Books I Have Read

Name of Book:		
....		AWARD
Author:	Date Read:	Sticker!

Name of Book:		
....		AWARD
Author:	Date Read:	Sticker!

The funniest book I ever read is:

_____

Name of Book:		
....		AWARD
Author:	Date Read:	Sticker!

Name of Book:		
....		AWARD
Author:	Date Read:	Sticker!

Books I Have Read

Name of Book:

....

Author:

Date Read:

AWARD
Sticker!

Name of Book:

....

Author:

Date Read:

AWARD
Sticker!

Name of Book:

....

Author:

Date Read:

AWARD
Sticker!

MARJORIE WEINMAN SHARMAT, the author of **Gila Monsters Meet You at the Airport** and the **Nate the Great** books, started writing when she was eight years old. While in elementary school, she and a friend "published" a newspaper called **The Snooper's Gazette** which was filled with news they got from spying on grownups.

P.L. TRAVERS, who wrote Mary Poppins, began writing when she was seven.

I wrote my first story when I was _____.

Books I Have Read

Name of Book:	
....	AWARD Sticker!
Author:	Date Read:

Name of Book:	
....	AWARD Sticker!
Author:	Date Read:

Name of Book:	
....	AWARD Sticker!
Author:	Date Read:

Name of Book:	
....	AWARD Sticker!
Author:	Date Read:

Name of Book:	
....	AWARD Sticker!
Author:	Date Read:

An illustrator is someone who draws or paints pictures. My favorite children's book

illustrator is: _____

Some of the books that this person has illustrated are: _____

_____

If I were an illustrator, I would make books with pictures of: _____

_____

Here is a picture I drew that I might put in a book someday.

Books I Have Read

Name of Book:

....

Author: Date Read:

AWARD
Sticker!

Name of Book:

....

Author: Date Read:

AWARD
Sticker!

Who wrote a book about a spider who could write?

_____

Name of Book:

....

Author: Date Read:

AWARD
Sticker!

Name of Book:

....

Author: Date Read:

AWARD
Sticker!

Books I Have Read

Name of Book:

....
Author: Date Read:

AWARD
Sticker!

Name of Book:

....
Author: Date Read:

AWARD
Sticker!

The scariest book I ever read is:

_____

Name of Book:

....
Author: Date Read:

AWARD
Sticker!

Name of Book:

....
Author: Date Read:

AWARD
Sticker!

Books I Have Read

Name of Book:

....

Author:

Date Read:

AWARD
Sticker!

Name of Book:

....

Author:

Date Read:

AWARD
Sticker!

So far I have read _____ books!

Name of Book:

....

Author:

Date Read:

AWARD
Sticker!

Name of Book:

....

Author:

Date Read:

AWARD
Sticker!

My favorite author is : _____

I like this writer very much because: _____

_____

_____

_____

Name of Book:

....
Author:

Date Read:

AWARD
Sticker!

Name of Book:

....
Author:

Date Read:

AWARD
Sticker!

Name of Book:

....
Author:

Date Read:

AWARD
Sticker!

Books I Have Read

Name of Book:
....

| Author: | Date Read: | AWARD Sticker! |

Name of Book:
....

| Author: | Date Read: | AWARD Sticker! |

Name of Book:
....

| Author: | Date Read: | AWARD Sticker! |

DR. SUESS'S real name is THEODOR S. GEISEL, and SAMUEL CLEMENS is the real name of MARK TWAIN. Sometimes authors use a "pen name" or "nom de plume" (nome-day-ploom) instead of using their own names. If you were to make up a pen name for your stories or poems, what would it be?

_____

Books I Have Read

Name of Book:

....

Author:

Date Read:

AWARD Sticker!

Name of Book:

....

Author:

Date Read:

AWARD Sticker!

If I were going to write a book, I would write one about: _____

_____

Name of Book:

....

Author:

Date Read:

AWARD Sticker!

Name of Book:

....

Author:

Date Read:

AWARD Sticker!

Books I Have Read

Name of Book:

....

Author:

Date Read:

AWARD
Sticker!

Name of Book:

....

Author:

Date Read:

AWARD
Sticker!

Name of Book:

....

Author:

Date Read:

AWARD
Sticker!

Name of Book:

....

Author:

Date Read:

AWARD
Sticker!

What is the name of a book about a curious little monkey and a man with a big yellow hat?

_____

Books I Have Read

Name of Book:

....

Author: Date Read:

AWARD
Sticker!

Name of Book:

....

Author: Date Read:

AWARD
Sticker!

So far I have read _____ books!

Name of Book:

....

Author: Date Read:

AWARD
Sticker!

Name of Book:

....

Author: Date Read:

AWARD
Sticker!

Books I Have Read

Name of Book:

....

Author:

Date Read:

AWARD
Sticker!

Name of Book:

....

Author:

Date Read:

AWARD
Sticker!

Name of Book:

....

Author:

Date Read:

AWARD
Sticker!

At one time ANITA LOBEL, author of **The Straw Maid**, **Sven's Bridge, The Pancake**, and many other books, wanted to be an actress. Today she uses the things she knows about the theatre to help her illustrate and write children's books. She also met her husband, children's author ARNOLD LOBEL, when she was cast in a play he was directing.

Books I Have Read

Name of Book:	
Author:	Date Read:	AWARD Sticker!

Name of Book:	
Author:	Date Read:	AWARD Sticker!

Name of Book:	
Author:	Date Read:	AWARD Sticker!

Name of Book:	
Author:	Date Read:	AWARD Sticker!

Name of Book:	
Author:	Date Read:	AWARD Sticker!

Books I Have Read

Name of Book:

....

Author:

Date Read:

AWARD
Sticker!

Name of Book:

....

Author:

Date Read:

AWARD
Sticker!

Name of Book:

....

Author:

Date Read:

AWARD
Sticker!

Name of Book:

....

Author:

Date Read:

AWARD
Sticker!

What is the name of a book about 12 little girls in two straight lines who lived in an old house in Paris that was covered in vines?

_____

Books I Have Read

Name of Book:

....

Author: Date Read:

```
AWARD
Sticker!
```

Name of Book:

....

Author: Date Read:

```
AWARD
Sticker!
```

My favorite place to read is: _____

_____

Name of Book:

....

Author: Date Read:

```
AWARD
Sticker!
```

Name of Book:

....

Author: Date Read:

```
AWARD
Sticker!
```

Books I Have Read

Name of Book:	
Author: .... Date Read:	AWARD Sticker!

Name of Book:	
Author: .... Date Read:	AWARD Sticker!

Name of Book:	
Author: .... Date Read:	AWARD Sticker!

Name of Book:	
Author: .... Date Read:	AWARD Sticker!

Name of Book:	
Author: .... Date Read:	AWARD Sticker!

Books I Have Read

Name of Book:

....

Author: Date Read:

AWARD Sticker!

Name of Book:

....

Author: Date Read:

AWARD Sticker!

So far I have read _____ books!

Name of Book:

....

Author: Date Read:

AWARD Sticker!

Name of Book:

....

Author: Date Read:

AWARD Sticker!

Books I Have Read

Name of Book:	
	AWARD Sticker!
Author:	
	Date Read:

Name of Book:	
	AWARD Sticker!
Author:	
	Date Read:

My favorite character in a book is:

_____

Name of Book:	
	AWARD Sticker!
Author:	
	Date Read:

Name of Book:	
	AWARD Sticker!
Author:	
	Date Read:

Books I Have Read

Name of Book:	
....	AWARD Sticker!
Author:	Date Read:	

Name of Book:	
....	AWARD Sticker!
Author:	Date Read:	

My favorite poet is: _____

Here is a poem I wrote.

_____

_____

_____

_____

Books I Have Read

Name of Book:	
....	AWARD Sticker!
Author:	Date Read:	

Name of Book:	
....	AWARD Sticker!
Author:	Date Read:	

The book I most like to have an adult read to me is:

_____

Name of Book:	
....	AWARD Sticker!
Author:	Date Read:	

Name of Book:	
....	AWARD Sticker!
Author:	Date Read:	

Books I Have Read

Name of Book:

....

Author: Date Read: AWARD Sticker!

Name of Book:

....

Author: Date Read: AWARD Sticker!

Name of Book:

....

Author: Date Read: AWARD Sticker!

A "collaboration" is when two or more people work together on a book. MITRA MODARRESSI, an illustrator, and her mother, author ANNE TYLER, "collaborated" on *Tumble Tower*. AUDREY and DON WOOD joined their separate talents (writing and painting) to make *The Napping House* and *King Bidgood's in the Bathtub*. If you have a parent or brother or sister who draws or paints, ask them to create pictures to go with something you have written. Or, if you're good at art, illustrate a story or a poem written by a friend who likes to write. Put both of your names on the cover and you will be a "collaborator" too.

Books I Have Read

Name of Book:

....

Author:

Date Read:

AWARD
Sticker!

Name of Book:

....

Author:

Date Read:

AWARD
Sticker!

Who wrote a book about a famous frog and toad?

_____

Name of Book:

....

Author:

Date Read:

AWARD
Sticker!

Name of Book:

....

Author:

Date Read:

AWARD
Sticker!

Books I Have Read

Name of Book:

....

Author: Date Read:

AWARD
Sticker!

Name of Book:

....

Author: Date Read:

AWARD
Sticker!

Name of Book:

....

Author: Date Read:

AWARD
Sticker!

LEO LIONNI has used mice as a kind of trademark character. His book **Frederick** is about a family of field mice. Can you name some other books that have mice as special characters?

_____

_____

Books I Have Read

Name of Book:

....

Author: Date Read: AWARD Sticker!

Name of Book:

....

Author: Date Read: AWARD Sticker!

Name of Book:

....

Author: Date Read: AWARD Sticker!

Name of Book:

....

Author: Date Read: AWARD Sticker!

I have read _____ books!

Help Your Child Become
A Lifelong Reader

Below are some simple ways of improving your child's reading skills and helping him to enjoy reading for a lifetime.

- Have your child practice reading aloud to you for 15 minutes a day; you will be amazed at the progress in only a few weeks.
- Continue to read aloud to your child, even after she has begun reading herself.
- Set aside a special time and place to read with one another, and make reading an important part of your day together.
- Let your child see YOU reading. Children of parents who read become readers themselves just as children of parents who watch television also do as the adults do.
- Regularly take your child to the local library and bookstore.
- Give your child books as special gifts and rewards.
- Help your child find reading material about his special interests.
- Have your child keep a written record of the books she has read.

GREAT BOOKS TO READ AND REREAD

I

BEGINNING READERS:
Ages 4 through 7

This category contains mostly picture and story books with simple texts and easy-to-grasp story lines. All are appropriate for reading aloud to younger children and were chosen to stimulate their interest in reading. These books are also suitable for children in the lower grades who have just begun to read. Many may begin with the easiest of "Easy Readers" such as **Go, Dog, Go** and then, as their skills increase, return with pleasure to a book such as **Harry the Dirty Dog**, which has been read to them for years.

❏ *Alexander and the Terrible, Horrible, No Good, Very Bad Day* by Judith Viorst
❏ *Amos and Boris* by William Steig
❏ *Anatole* by Eve Titus
❏ *The Bee Tree* by Patricia Polacco
❏ *Bently & egg* by William Joyce
❏ *Blueberries for Sal* by Robert McCloskey
❏ *Bread and Jam for Frances* by Russell Hoban
❏ *Bringing the Rain to Kapiti Plain: A Nandi Tale* by Verna Aardema
❏ *The Cat in the Hat* by Dr. Seuss
❏ *A Chair for My Mother* by Vera B. Williams
❏ *Cherries and Cherry Pits* by Vera B. Williams
❏ *Cloudy With a Chance of Meatballs* by Judith Barrett
❏ *Corduroy* by Don Freeman
❏ *Could be Worse!* by James Stevenson
❏ *The Country Bunny and the Little Gold Shoes* by DuBose Heyward
❏ *Curious George* by H.A. Rey
❏ *Days with Frog and Toad* by Arnold Lobel
❏ *Do Not Open* by Brinton Turkle
❏ *The Dream Pillow* by Mitra Modarressi
❏ *Each Peach Pear Plum* by Janet and Allen Ahlberg
❏ *The Fool of the World and the Flying Ship* by Arthur Ransome
❏ *Frederick* by Leo Lionni

❏ *Frog and Toad Together* by Arnold Lobel

❏ *George and Martha* by James Marshall

❏ *The Giant Jam Sandwich* by John Vernon Lord and Janet Burroway

❏ *Go, Dog, Go* by P.D. Eastman

❏ *Goggles!* by Ezra Jack Keats

❏ *Grandfather's Journey* by Allen Say

❏ *The Great Blueness and Other Predicaments* by Arnold Lobel

❏ *Hansy's Mermaid* by Trinka Hakes Noble

❏ *Harry the Dirty Dog* by Gene Zion

❏ *Heckedy Peg* by Audrey Wood

❏ *A House is a House for Me* by Mary Ann Hoberman

❏ *The House on East 88th Street* by Bernard Waber

❏ *How the Manx Cat Lost Its Tail* by Janet Stevens

❏ *If You Give a Moose a Muffin* by Laura Joffe Numeroff

❏ *Ira Sleeps Over* by Bernard Waber

❏ *I Want a Dog* by Dayal Kaur Khalsa

❏ *King Bidgood's in the Bathtub* by Audrey Wood

❏ *The Lady with the Ship on Her Head* by Deborah Nourse Lattimore

❏ *Little Bear* by Else Holmelund Minarik

❏ *The Little House* by Virginia Lee Burton

❏ *Lon Po Po: A Red-Riding Hood Story from China* by Ed Young

❏ *Louis the Fish* by Arthur Yorinks

❏ *Lyle, Lyle, Crocodile* by Bernard Waber

❏ *Madeline* by Ludwig Bemelmans

❏ *Make Way for Ducklings* by Robert McCloskey

❏ *Many Moons* by James Thurber

❏ *Millions of Cats* by Wanda Gag

❏ *Ming Lo Moves the Mountain* by Arnold Lobel

❏ *Miss Nelson Is Missing* by Harry Allard

❏ *Miss Rumphius* by Barbara Cooney

❏ *The Mitten* by Jan Brett

❏ *Mr. Rabbit and the Lovely Present* by Charlotte Zolotow

❏ *Music, Music Everywhere* by Vera B. Williams

❏ *The Napping House* by Audrey Wood

❏ *Neighbors* by M.B. Goffstein

❏ *A New Coat for Anna* by Harriet Ziefert

- ❏ *The Ox-Cart Man* by Donald Hall
- ❏ *The Pancake* by Anita Lobel
- ❏ *Peppe the Lamplighter* by Elisa Bartone
- ❏ *The Philharmonic Gets Dressed* by Karla Kushkin
- ❏ *The Polar Express* by Chris Van Allsburg
- ❏ *Princess Furball* by Charlotte Huck
- ❏ *The Purple Coat* by Amy Hest
- ❏ *Richard Scarry's What Do People Do All Day?* by Richard Scarry
- ❏ *Rumpelstiltskin Retold* by Paul Galdon
- ❏ *The Seven Chinese Brothers* by Margaret Mahy
- ❏ *Sing a Song of Popcorn: Every Child's Book of Poems* Compiled by Beatrice Schenk de Regniers
- ❏ *Six Darn Cows* by Margaret Laurence
- ❏ *The Snowy Day* by Ezra Jack Keats
- ❏ *Song and Dance Man* by Karen Ackerman
- ❏ *Stellaluna* by Janell Cannon
- ❏ *Stone Soup* by Marcia Brown
- ❏ *The Story About Ping* by Marjorie Flack
- ❏ *The Story of Ferdinand* by Munro Leaf
- ❏ *Strega Nona* by Tomie de Paola
- ❏ *Sylvester and the Magic Pebble* by William Steig
- ❏ *The Tale of Peter Rabbit* by Beatrix Potter
- ❏ *Tell Me a Mitzi* by Lore Segal
- ❏ *Those Terrible Toy-Breakers* by David McPhail
- ❏ *Three Big Hogs* by Manus Pinkwater
- ❏ *A Three Hat Day* by Laura Geringer
- ❏ *Thunder Cake* by Patricia Polacco
- ❏ *Tikki Tikki Tembo* by Arlene Mosel
- ❏ *The Twelve Dancing Princesses Retold* by Freya Littledale
- ❏ *The Vingananee and the Tree Toad* by Verna Aardema
- ❏ *Tree of Cranes* by Allen Say
- ❏ *The Tsar and the Amazing Cow* by J. Patrick Lewis
- ❏ *Uncle Jed's Barbershop* by Margaree King Mitchell
- ❏ *What's the Matter with Carruthers? A Bedtime Story* by James Marshall
- ❏ *When We Were Young* by A.A. Milne
- ❏ *The Wonderful Shrinking Shirt* by Leone Castell Anderson
- ❏ *You Be Good and I'll Be Night: Jump-on-the-Bed Poems* by Eve Merriam

II

PROGRESSING YOUNG READERS:
Ages 5 through 9

There are still a number of picture and story books here, but they contain more sophisticated language and plots and often deal with historical events and real people. Many of the other books listed are termed "Easy Readers" by librarians and are excellent sources for quickly progressing younger readers. There are also a few books, such as **Ramona the Pest** and **Mrs. Piggle Wiggle**, which contain longer text but are on a level that this age group of children will enjoy.

❏ *The Amazing Bone* by William Steig
❏ *Amelia Bedelia* by Peggy Parish
❏ *And Then What Happened, Paul Revere?* by Jean Fritz
❏ *Annie and the Old One* by Miska Miles
❏ *Arthur's Prize Reader* by Lillian Hoban
❏ *"B" Is for Betsy* by Carolyn Haywood
❏ *Blue Moose* by Manus Pinkwater
❏ *Bony-Legs* by Joanna Cole
❏ *Brave Irene* by William Steig
❏ *Caleb and Kate* by William Steig
❏ *A Child's Garden of Verses* by Robert Louis Stevenson
❏ *Chin Chiang and the Dragon's Dance* by Ian Wallace
❏ *The Church Mouse* by Graham Oakley
❏ *d'Aulaires' Book of Greek Myths* by Ingri and Edgar d'Aulaire
❏ *Dawn* by Molly Bang
❏ *Digging Up Dinosaurs* by Aliki
❏ *Duffy and the Devil* by Harve and Margot Zemach
❏ *Emily* by Michael Bedard
❏ *The Enormous Crocodile* by Roald Dahl
❏ *Eyes of the Dragon* by Margaret Leaf
❏ *Fast and Slow, Poems* by John Ciardi
❏ *Fast Friends, Two Stories* by James Stevenson
❏ *The 500 Hats of Bartholomew Cubbin* by Dr. Seuss

❑ *The Forgetful Wishing Well: Poems for Young People*
   by X.J. Kennedy

❑ *Fox All Week* by Edward Marshall

❑ *Fox and His Friends* by Edward Marshall

❑ *Fox Song* by Joseph Bruchac

❑ *The Giving Tree* by Shel Silverstein

❑ *The Gollywhopper Egg* by Anne Rockwell

❑ *Griselda's New Year* by Marjorie Weinman Sharmat

❑ *Harold and the Giant Knight* by Donald Carrick

❑ *Higglety Piggelty Pop: Or, There Must Be More to Life*
   by Maurice Sendak

❑ *How My Parents Learned to Eat* by Ina R. Friedman

❑ *How Pizza Came to Queens* by Dayal Kaur Khalsa

❑ *Jane Martin, Dog Detective* by Eve Bunting

❑ *The Judge* by Harve Zemach

❑ *Keep the Lights Burning, Abbie* by Peter and Connie Roop

❑ *Little House in the Big Woods* by Laura Ingalls Wilder

❑ *The Magic Finger* by Roald Dahl

❑ *The Magic School Bus At the Waterworks* by Joanna Cole

❑ *The Magic School Bus Inside the Earth* by Joanna Cole

❑ *The Magic School Bus Inside the Human Body* by Joanna Cole

❑ *The Magic School Bus On the Ocean Floor* by Joanna Cole

❑ *The Man Who Could Call Down Owls* by Eve Bunting

❑ *Marie Curie* by Ibi Lepscky

❑ *Morris and Boris, Three Stories* by Bernard Wiseman

❑ *Mouse Tales* by Arnold Lobel

❑ *Mr. Popper's Penguins* by Richard and Florence Atwater

❑ *Mrs. Piggle-Wiggle* By Betty MacDonald

❑ *Mufaro's Beautiful Daughters: An African Tale* by John Steptoe

❑ *My New York* by Kathy Jakobsen

❑ *Nate the Great* by Marjorie Weinman Sharmat

❑ *Nate the Great and the Sticky Case* by Marjorie Weinman Sharmat

❑ *Nate the Great Goes Undercover* by Marjorie Weinman Sharmat

❑ *The New Kid on the Block* by Jack Prelutsky

❑ *Nobody's Cat* by Miska Miles

❑ *Now We Are Six* by A.A. Milne

❑ *Owl at Home* by Arnold Lobel

GREAT BOOKS TO READ AND REREAD

- ❏ *Pink and Say* by Patricia Polacco
- ❏ *Ramona Quimby, Age 8* by Beverly Cleary
- ❏ *Ramona the Pest* by Beverly Cleary
- ❏ *The Rough-Face Girl* by Rafe Martin
- ❏ *Sam the Minuteman* by Nathaniel Benchley
- ❏ *Sarah Morton's Day: A Day in the Life of a Pilgrim Girl* by Kate Waters
- ❏ *Shaka, King of the Zulus* by Diane Stanley and Peter Vennema
- ❏ *Snow Lion* by David McPhail
- ❏ *Soul Looks Back in Wonder* by Tom Feelings
- ❏ *Stevie* by John Steptoe
- ❏ *The Story of the Statue of Liberty* by Betsy and Giulio Maestro
- ❏ *Sukey and the Mermaid* by Robert D. San Souci
- ❏ *Tales of Amanda Pig* by Jean Van Leeuwen
- ❏ *Tales of a Gambling Grandma* by Dayal Kaur Khalsa
- ❏ *The Talking Eggs* by Robert D. San Souci
- ❏ *There is a Carrot in My Ear and Other Noodle Tales* by Alvin Schwartz
- ❏ *Two Laughable Lyrics* by Edward Lear
- ❏ *Tye May and the Magic Brush* by Molly Bang
- ❏ *Uncle Elephant* by Arnold Lobel
- ❏ *The Velveteen Rabbit, Original Text* by Margery Williams
- ❏ *The Wall* by Eve Bunting
- ❏ *The Way I Feel...Sometimes* by Beatrice Schenk de Regniers
- ❏ *The Wednesday Surprise* by Eve Bunting
- ❏ *What's the Big Idea, Ben Franklin?* by Jean Fritz
- ❏ *Who's Afraid of Ernestine?* by Marjorie Weinman Sharmat
- ❏ *Where the Sidewalk Ends: Poems and Drawings* by Shel Silverstein
- ❏ *You Read to Me, I'll Read to You* by John Ciardi

III

ADVANCED READERS
Ages 8-12

Readers of this group are ready for what is often thought of as the heart of children's literature — a rich mixture of myths, mysteries, chapter books, adventures, poetry, and enduring stories about other cultures and earlier times. Although the books here certainly contain more sophisticated plots and language than earlier ones, they rarely deal with the coming-of-age and self-awareness themes that appear in young adult novels. Most of these books are also excellent for reading aloud to attentive younger children.

❏ *Abel's Island* by William Steig
❏ *The Adventures of Pinocchio* by Carlo Collodi
❏ *All-of-a-Kind Family* by Sidney Taylor
❏ *The Animal Family* by Randall Jarrell
❏ *Anne of Green Gables* by L.M. Montgomery
❏ *Around the World in Eighty Days* by Jules Verne
❏ *Baseball in April* by Gary Soto
❏ *The Bat-Poet* by Randall Jarrell
❏ *Behind the Attic Wall* by Sylvia Cassedy
❏ *The Best Christmas Pageant Ever* by Barbara Robinson
❏ *The BFG* by Roald Dahl
❏ *Black Beauty* by Anna Sewell
❏ *Blue Willow* by Doris Gates
❏ *The Borrowers* by Mary Norton
❏ *The Brave Little Toaster* by Thomas M. Disch
❏ *Charlie and the Chocolate Factory* by Roald Dahl
❏ *Charlotte's Web* by E.B. White
❏ *A Child's Christmas in Wales* by Dylan Thomas
❏ *Chocolate Fever* by Robert Kimmel Smith
❏ *A Christmas Carol* by Charles Dickens
❏ *The Chronicles of Narnia* by C.S. Lewis
❏ *Clever Gretchen and Other Forgotten Folktales* by Alison Lurie
❏ *Come Sing, Jimmy Jo* by Katherine Paterson

GREAT BOOKS TO READ AND REREAD

❏ *The Cricket in Times Square* by George Selden
❏ *Danny the Champion of the World* by Roald Dahl
❏ *Dear Mr. Henshaw* by Beverly Cleary
❏ *The Disappearance of Sister Perfect* by Jill Pinkwater
❏ *The Doll's House* by Rumer Godden
❏ *The Egypt Game* by Zilpha Keatley Snyder
❏ *Einstein Anderson, Science Sleuth* by Seymour Simon
❏ *Five Children and It* by E. Nesbit
❏ *The Fledgling* by Jane Langton
❏ *Freaky Friday* by Mary Rogers
❏ *Ginger Pye* by Eleanor Estes
❏ *The Girl Who Cried Flowers and Other Tales* by Jane Yolen
❏ *Goldie the Dollmaker* by M.B. Goffstein
❏ *The Great Gilly Hopkins* by Katharine Paterson
❏ *The Hobbit* by J.R.R. Tolkein
❏ *The House with a Clock in Its Walls* by John Bellairs
❏ *The Hundred Dresses* by Eleanor Estes
❏ *Hurry Home, Candy* by Meindert DeJong
❏ *Ida Early Comes Over the Mountain* by Robert Burch
❏ *Island of the Blue Dolphins* by Scott O'Dell
❏ *In the Year of the Boar and Jackie Robinson* by Bette Bao Lord
❏ *James and the Giant Peach* by Roald Dahl
❏ *Jump! The Adventures of Brer Rabbit* by Van Dyke Parks and
  Malcolm Jones
❏ *Just So Stories* by Rudyard Kipling
❏ *Kneeknock Rise* by Natalie Babbitt
❏ *Lassie-Come-Home* by Eric Knight
❏ *The Last of the Mohicans* by James Fenimore Cooper
❏ *The Light in the Attic* by Shel Silverstein
❏ *The Lion, the Witch and the Wardrobe* by C.S. Lewis
❏ *Little Town on the Prairie* by Laura Ingalls Wilder
❏ *Little Women* by Louisa May Alcott
❏ *The Lost Umbrella of Kim Chu* by Eleanor Estes
❏ *The Moffats* by Eleanor Estes
❏ *National Velvet* by Enid Bagnold
❏ *One-Eyed Cat* by Paula Fox
❏ *The Olden Days Coat* by Margaret Laurence
❏ *The People Could Fly* by Virginia Hamilton

Great Books to Read and Reread

- *Peter Pan* by J.M. Barrie
- *Pippi Longstocking* by Astrid Lingren
- *Rabbit Hill* by Robert Lawson
- *The Rainbow People* by Laurence Yep
- *Roll of Thunder, Hear My Cry* by Mildred Taylor
- *Rootabaga Stories* by Carl Sandburg
- *Sarah, Plain and Tall* by Patricia MacLachlan
- *Scary Stories to Tell in the Dark: Collected from American Folklore* by Alvin Schwartz
- *The Search for Delicious* by Natalie Babbitt
- *The Secret Garden* by Frances Hodgson Burnett
- *The Secret Language* by Ursula Nordstrom
- *The Sign of the Beaver* by Elizabeth George Speare
- *Skinnybones* by Barbara Park
- *Sounder* by William H. Armstrong
- *Soup* by Robert Newton Peck
- *Stories for Children* by Isaac Bashevis Singer
- *The Story of Doctor Doolittle* (revised edition) by Hugh Lofting
- *The Story of King Arthur and His Knights* by Howard Pyle
- *Stuart Little* by E.B. White
- *Thank You, Jackie Robinson* by Barbara Cohen
- *The 13 Clocks* by James Thurber
- *Heidi* by Johanna Spyri
- *Treasure Island* by Robert Louis Stevenson
- *The Trumpet of the Swan* by E.B. White
- *Tuck Everlasting* by Natalie Babbitt
- *Two Piano Tuners* by M.B. Goffstein
- *Watership Down* by Richard Adams
- *The Wind in the Willows* by Kenneth Grahame
- *Winnie-the-Pooh* by A.A. Milne
- *The Wonderful Wizard of Oz* by L. Frank Baum
- *The Yearling* by Marjorie Kinnan Rawlings